Praise for *Yes, I CAN*

"Carmela brings tremendous insight and discernment regarding leadership, especially as it relates to women. She combines a gift for teaching and communicating with a passion for helping women to create a highly effective message which is beneficial to all who have the privilege of learning from her. She has much to offer in the way of helping women realize their full God-given potential!"

– Kellie Agulia, Women's Ministry Coordinator
Stuart Campus, Christ Fellowship

"Carmela Kirk has been a mentor, friend, and fan of mine for over five years now. She is rich in character and strong in spirit. Carmela offers great wisdom and enthusiastic encouragement to women encountering difficult times. She is able to offer a new and fresh perspective to encourage personal growth. My personal experience was quite intense, yet Carmela dove in fully willing to assist me on a path to know the Lord's true desire and purpose for me. She has a gentle yet persistent approach to ensure accountability for bettering oneself. I am grateful for the wonderful opportunity to have worked, and still work with Carmela."

– Ashley Horn, RN Martin County, FL

"Carmela's warm and transparent teachings leave the listener/ reader wanting more. Using some of her own experiences makes one able to easily identify and apply scripture to daily living! She's been a true blessing to our leadership team!"

– Kathy Palmer
Christ Fellowship Church Member/Leadership Team

"Today I am a confident woman knowing who I am in Christ Jesus. There was a time I thought I needed to perform and do everything perfectly. I always fell short and frozen in fear. I am so grateful to Christ Fellowship and the many life groups, Carmela and Higher pursuits for women. God said we were never meant to do life alone. In sharing with other Christian women my shortcomings/character defects....I can fight against them and know that Christ loves me just the way I am!!! Thankful to God for bringing this group and all the many women together to stand strong in our walk with Christ Jesus."

– Kim Beckett
Christ Fellowship Church Member/Leadership Team

Yes, I CAN

Become the Woman
I Was Created to Be

CARMELA KIRK

one way
PUBLISHING

One Way Publishing, LLC
OneWayWriter.com

Ordering Information:
Quantity sales. Special discounts are available on quantity purchases by
corporations, associations, and others. For details, contact the publisher at
the address above.
Orders by U.S. trade bookstores and wholesalers. Please contact Lightning
Source, or Spring Arbor

Book design by Maureen Cutajar
www.gopublished.com

Printed in the United States of America
ISBN: 978-0970726261

First Edition
14   13   12   11   10   /   10   9   8   7   6   5   4   3   2   1

As you begin this journey, it is my prayer that your spirit is filled with peace, joy and a sense of complete freedom.

~Carmela

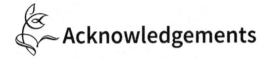# Acknowledgements

While writing this book, I kept getting interrupted. It just wasn't right and I would have to switch gears; something was incomplete. I wanted to write a nice safe "how to get healthy" book, but God had other plans. I will forever be grateful to my Father for His patience with me while nudging me incessantly and using my pain and growth for His good.

I humbly thank Him for Christ Fellowship church where we study, grow and serve; where my husband has learned to be the leader God created him to be.

This book never would have come about without Jessica Gaffney's intuition and encouragement. Patrice Kelty, you are so talented and gifted, I'm so grateful for your help.

Thank you to my husband and best friend who has stood beside me with never ending patience and support.

Chelsea and Alex, you gave me permission to go for it. I will always be your greatest fan and I am ridiculously proud of both of you.

MaryAnn, you have been an ever present voice of encouragement, I look forward to all the future adventures God has in store for us. Rosanna, you changed my life, you taught me how to connect the dots and I will be forever grateful.

Lastly, I want to thank my mom, who has role modeled exactly how to be a woman of integrity, grace and humble servant hood.

Contents

 **Foreword**

Our world needs better moms, better role models, better wives, who understand that it's okay to struggle and learn from mistakes. How can we warn our daughters what a man looks like that is preying on her vulnerability if we don't admit we fell for his compliments and attention? How can we warn our daughters that it is not okay to compromise our principles for anyone, if they don't know the consequences of what happened when we did?

I haven't had all of the experiences needed to teach our daughters everything they need to know; I need you and your story. Let's be honest, this world is getting crazier by the minute. You don't have to write a book or even make your struggles public, I'm just encouraging you to be real. Join me and speak love into our daughters and sisters. Let her know she has a voice, she has support, she is not alone, she does not have to be perfect and she is beautifully made.

What good is it if a young woman looks at me and sees a confident, secure, happy, successful leader? How much better if she looks at me and knows I've been broken, I've made mistakes and have been lost but have found the way out and not only survived but thrived. Way better...

Our Story

Tom and I were high school sweethearts. He sat behind me in history class our junior year. Instead of paying attention to the teacher, I would often daydream about the future. I caught myself, on more than one occasion thinking, "if I were going to marry anyone, it would be someone like Tom Kirk."

He was a confident yet quiet teenager with nothing to prove to anyone. I liked that. He was (and is) the kind of guy that held the door for you, he didn't swear and he treated girls with respect. We had a blast when I was on the gymnastics team and he was a wrestler. Our teams worked out in the same gym and the coaches had the hardest time making us pay attention to our workouts instead of each other.

After high school graduation I traveled overseas, and he went to school in another state but we always seemed to make it work. My family loved him. When you take a 16 year old boy who relied on no one and put him into my big Italian female-dominated household, it was meant to be.

We married when we were 23 years old and, like most kids, we each had our own expectations. Like many, we did not take into account the fact that our role models for marriage and family were totally different. My family did not want me to stray too far from the nest while his encouraged total and complete independence.

My Italian family is intimately intertwined with each other and I did not see the impact or problem with involving them in my marriage. Tom, however, was expecting us to have a more private relationship. I had a need for interaction with my sisters that Tom could not understand. He was the logical problem solver and I was the emotional, relational person in our marriage.

Stubbornly, I held tight to my ideology of a happy marriage and when things turned out to be less than perfect, I refused to admit that there was a problem. As time wore on and the newness wore off, we drifted. Instead of talking about how I felt and admitting I was unhappy, I took matters into my own hands and looked for satisfaction outside the marriage.

Substance and alcohol use, flirting, intense binges of working, abusing exercise, abusing food -- all of these behaviors helped me escape and avoid my feelings. I thought my feelings of discontent were unwarranted; I acted as if how I felt in the relationship was not important. To me, what was important was how Tom felt and how well he was doing. Tom knew how to take care of himself, so he did. There were plenty of happy times but the unhappy times we did not manage well.

Something inside me wasn't right. I had this feeling in the back of my mind that something was wrong. I knew I wasn't coping well, so when I sought help and we learned some early recovery principles, it helped. Unfortunately, it was still uncomfortable to address any real issues. Those issues, we avoided, escaped and didn't talk about. So it was almost like we took two steps forward and one back. When we got a little better, we thought we were all better. It was time to have children!

Chelsea was born and flipped our world upside down. We never imagined we could love someone this much! When she was 8 months old, while working in the ER, I called my doctor and told him I was not feeling well. I ordered some blood work on myself (which you could do in those days) and the doctor insisted I get a pregnancy test. I reminded him "No, I have a baby and I cannot possibly be pregnant; I'm still breastfeeding!" (That would be a good example of my denial and control issues), but he asked me to "pretend I'm the doctor, Carmela and do what I say".

I complied and whoa, the pregnancy test was positive! I had two children 15 months apart. Chelsea, who at three years old, told me "Mom, if you do what I say we will get along just fine," and Alex who when asked at four years old if anyone made fun of his lisp (because they were) said "why would anyone make fun of me? I'm a cool guy." I think that sums up each of their personalities the best. Of course, I adored my children and still do. Unfortunately, with their lives being so cared for, Tom and I came last. How I wish I could have a do over for this stage of my life. The kids have mostly happy, stable memories. The pain and suffering I endured was primarily on the inside, and between us as a couple.

My father died very suddenly when the kids were still young. This sudden loss, accompanied by a dysfunctional marriage, financial hardship and daily disappointment, sent us into our next move. Tom rightly believed a move to Florida would improve his chances of promotion and be good for the family. I however, felt alone and would greatly miss my family.

With this move to Florida, although Tom's work life would improve, I sunk deeper into depression. I found many friends and there were lots of fun, happy times, but again when the going got tough, we crumbled. In hindsight, we were missing a stable foundation, we had nowhere to turn for help and all we knew how to do was party to feel good or avoid and bury our feelings.

Tom was raised as a Christian and understood everything except forgiveness. When he could not be perfect for God, he ran and hid for many years. I was raised Catholic and although I knew and loved God, I was guilt ridden, always struggling to be better and never free. I struggled with just being honest about how I was feeling and what was going on inside of me. I was really good at denial, self-punishment and escaping into whichever behavior worked at the time. We had tried to take the kids to various churches but could never connect and could never get on the same page at the same time.

We finally reached bottom. The kids were middle school age and they too were starting to behave like many other adolescents. Our family was not a family any more; we were four people living four different lives hanging on by a thread. There was not a lot of fighting or conflict – there was none, but that was worse. There was absolute and total unhappiness and no one was talking about it.

Tom and I had to get very real with each other and we both agreed it was over. We explained to our two beautiful children that things would be better if we were apart. They said they understood and insisted they were fine. They said it was important that we were both happy, and they wanted us to be happy. I guess that's what we wrongly believed too. We knew splitting up was not what was best for the family, but there was so much damage done in the relationship that we didn't think there was an option.

We were separated for three long years. After the first year, we were still lost. Even though I jumped right back into all of the recovery principles with both feet and was getting better; WE were lost. Even though he sought outside counsel and began addressing his own patterns and strongholds; WE were not okay. What most people did when a marriage ended- acting out, fighting, revenge- didn't work. How do you put a marriage back together that didn't work in the first place? After the second year, we lost hope. We got along wonderfully as friends and co-parents. We were both realizing and admitting our own parts in the break up. We tried to reconcile but quickly slipped back into complete dysfunction.

In reality we were losing our home, our family was dying and it seemed like there was absolutely no way out.

I began attending church. Tom was living thirty minutes away and began attending a satellite ministry connected to my church. Neither of us knew what the other was up to. Every week we were hearing the same message. With time and slowly putting one right foot after the other, it started to piece together.

We took a marriage class together and when the facilitator asked why God wants us to marry I answered "because we are sinners and He wants to punish us". How embarrassing, but that was how I felt! Tom and I have laughed about that night; because that was the night we got back together.

After three years of waiting and not knowing, we reconciled in one night. I hope you understand clearly. I'm sharing this story because we didn't do anything right. This is not about us – it is about what God did in us and for us. We were not capable of putting this marriage back. Please hear me.

I have no idea what it was or what specific thing was said that we hadn't already heard, but we both knew. We were back. We were back and things were going to be a lot different. We were going to put God first and foremost in the middle of it all. It wasn't suddenly easy and light from that point forward, but we had direction and we had a path to follow, but most of all we had God. We understood.

God made us man and woman, different but two equal halves to make one. Because of what Jesus did for us on the cross, we were complete. When Jesus rose from the dead and went to Heaven, He left us with the power of the Holy Spirit. We had somewhere to get our answers; we had a safe place to bring all our hurts and concerns. We were free to live a life that our Creator planned for us, not one that we were trying to put together from our own good ideas and unrealistic dreams.

Our story continues, like yours, every day. We have corrected that mistake in our thinking that the goal of life is to be happy. Ours is not a unique journey. I know so many people that have turned their lives over to the care of our loving Father and watched in amazement as it unfolded better than they could have imagined.

I share my story not because it is ground breaking, but because during my writing, I was called to share it. God wanted to use what we went through for His good. What else were we supposed to say except the only thing that has consistently worked so far – YES, LORD.

Fall and Die or Jump and Fly

The Day I Died

Throughout my childhood I had a recurring dream. In this dream, I saw my older self in a beautiful white dress while sitting on the attic floor in our old farmhouse. There was a window beside me, offering a cool breeze on what seemed to be a beautiful fall day. I remember hearing the laughter of children below me, and I knew instantly that they were mine.

At the sound of their giggles, I am overwhelmed with great love. As I sit there organizing my family's belongings, there is a mix of emotion. In my dream I know I am preparing to die and yet I feel a deep assurance that everything will be okay. The sense of peace I felt in that dream was heavenly.

For years I tried to understand what that dream meant. When I married and had children I often wondered if the dream meant that I would die at a young age. That was a powerful thought that almost derailed me. I understand now that it was a foretelling of what my future held.

This understanding came a few years in August, the 28th day to be exact. Similar to my dream, I was sitting in my favorite room of my beautiful house. I shared this home with my husband and two children. In my eyes I saw the parallel to my childhood dream, the beautiful home, the successful career, a handsome husband, two great kids; all the bells and whistles of success in today's culture. In my heart I knew the truth.

In spite of the outward appearances, my life was a mess. I sat on the floor and reality crashed in my face. I was assaulted by truth. I was assaulted by the secrets, the lies, the parties, the "fun," the little indiscretions here and there. I spent years lying to myself, telling myself I was happy, that nothing was wrong. I spent years justifying my behavior because it allowed me to escape reality. It allowed me to ignore my crumbling marriage, my insane drive for perfection and acceptance, and my unquenchable thirst for "approval."

I thought I lost my mind as I sat there sobbing uncontrollably. Everything was a lie. There was no happiness. It was dark and lonely. I saw all of my guilt, shame and sin. I couldn't catch my breath. I sat there gasping for air between sobs. Tears pouring from me as every bit of my body wept for what should have been. I wept for my lost dreams and unmet expectations. I wept for my father who passed away. I wept for my children who would soon endure a divorce.

While I sat there sobbing in my pit, I heard someone say, "Woman, why do you cry?" I was so emotional I didn't feel spooked by the voice; I felt comforted. Then I heard it again, "Woman, why do you cry?"

Immediately, I stopped crying. The voice was not really a voice, it was more of a thought that was not my own. While I had never heard anything like that, I knew right away that it was Jesus. How could that be? How could and why would Jesus want to talk with me? While I accepted Him in my heart years before, I certainly wasn't walking out my relationship with Him.

I hung my head in shame, afraid of His presence. I felt so unworthy. But here He was comforting me. His compassion spoke so loud and clear. Encountering Jesus was not what I expected. He did not remind me of my sin; in fact, He gently reminded me that I would need to die in order to live, but by doing so I would live more abundantly.

Isn't it wonderful to know He receives us just as we are?

At that moment I knew I had a choice. I could fall off of this self-imposed cliff or I could jump and fly; hanging on the edge was no longer an option.

If I fell off the cliff, the collateral damage to my family would be unbearable. If I jumped and flew off the cliff, I might be able to save the remnants, but flying takes work. It takes a lot of work.

On that fateful day in August, my Savior met me in the pit and He gave me the courage to admit my pain and face the consequences of my choices. I chose to trust a God that I hardly knew and try real faith for the first time. I didn't become the woman I was supposed to become. Where did I go wrong? The decision to change was hard and scary. Doubt plagued me. What if I fail? What if I can't change and I keep making wrong choices? What if I just keep making mistakes? What if it hurts too much?

My husband and I separated to avoid doing further damage to each other and our children, who were old enough to understand what was happening. We both sought outside counsel to work on our 'issues,' but at that time, I thought for sure divorce was imminent. The thought of divorce broke my heart, but I did not think there was an option. I had to fix myself. I had to find peace. I had to revive my spirit and learn to live again.

I won't lie; it was a painful journey. I joined a recovery program that helped me identify patterns that kept me in bondage and led me to sabotage my marriage, my health and my life.

On this journey, I had to forgive others and myself, but I also had to accept forgiveness. I had to learn to love myself and be honest about my choices, my feelings and my expectations. I had to stop hiding in perfectionism, food, alcohol, avoidance and people pleasing. This was a big change for me. Some days were overwhelming and 'felt' hopeless. I had to learn that it was okay; I was doing a lot better than I was feeling. Feeling better came later.

At some point I turned to the Bible, not for comfort or direction, but for a loophole that would justify a divorce. Instead I received comfort and direction to become a better wife and mother. One of the first verses someone pointed out, simply because the date was 8/28 was *Romans 8:28 "And we know that God causes everything to work together for the good of those who love God and are called according to His purpose for them."* This was it. This was God telling me that He would use the pain of my choices for His good. While it took some time, I learned that I didn't have to be afraid; He had a good plan for me.

Over the course of three years, God stripped me of my self-imposed defects. He changed me. He removed my heart of stone and gave me a new heart. And, while He worked on me, He worked on my husband.

During our separation, both my husband and I took the time apart to get healthy spiritually, emotionally and physically. We intended to divorce. In fact, over the three years, each of us served papers on the other, but when it came time to sign them something always came up to keep it from happening.

I am so grateful that we were never able to finalize the divorce. In fact, while God was working on us, we each found our own intimate relationship with God. We learned to love ourselves, which in turn, enabled us to love the other the way God intended for us to love. Thankfully, we were able to stand against society's idea of love, marriage and commitment.

Once I learned, and truly accepted, what Jesus did for me (and you) and understood that it is by grace that we are saved, I could accept the gift. The gift of freedom to reach out to a loving Father, to walk daily with our brother and live constantly with the Holy Spirit who is a spirit of power, love and self-discipline. That young girl from my dream didn't die; she was saved, healed and set free.

My path is narrow, but clear. My perfectionism, self-centeredness, codependence, isolation, anger, fear, and the need to escape are uncomfortable places now. I have nothing to fear. *Jeremiah 29:11 "For I know the plans I have for you," declares the Lord. "Plans to prosper you and not to harm you, plans to give you hope and a future."* Receive that! There is hope and a future!

I invite you to join me on the journey of a lifetime. We will take a journey of growth, healing and awareness. This journey will enable you to realize your full potential and embrace the power and beauty you possess.

God wants what is best for you. Are you willing to do the work?

This journey works best if you journal. Journaling will empower you to release the baggage of your past. It brings your pain into God's light where it belongs. This self-awareness will bring freedom, peace and joy. Once you remove this baggage, you will be free to experience life's great adventures fearlessly.

If you, like me, are afraid of putting your pain in writing, I encourage you to do it anyway. Fear is not from God. Fear will keep you in prison. Pick up your pen, answer the questions openly and honestly, then burn it if you have to. Just do it. Jump and Fly! Be encouraged, my friend. Flying healed the hurts of the past. Flying brought my family back.

When my children, husband and I are sitting around laughing about something or being goofy, I think about how close I came to losing it all. I thank God for the courage to face my pain and the grace to receive His healing.

There is a time and a season for all things. This is your time for healing, your time to learn to fly and to trust God.

All of this is scripture based and each chapter brings us closer to God because it teaches us to grow through and remove our obstacles.

If and when you choose to follow God, to study Him, to really let him in, make it deliberate and conscious and of your own free will. God created us to be in relationship with Him. He wants to guide us and walk closely with us, but first we must choose Him. If you have not yet done so, and you are reading this book, God is speaking to you. Pray this now: "God I want to get to know You. Reveal Yourself to me. Let me feel Your presence and hear Your voice." Now, hush child, you just spoke to your Creator... you just hush.

Imagine what it would be like to have direct access to the Creator of the universe. Not only access, but to have His loving, caring support and guidance. **Imagine** the power behind this kind of life. **Imagine** the possibilities!

 **Surrender**

Sometimes we find ourselves on a path that we never intended on taking and end up in a place we never thought we would be. If you find yourself at the bottom of the pit, congratulations! You have nowhere to go but up! Life is a series of mountain tops and valleys. Some valleys may be long, dark and cold, but they always lead to the mountain top if you keep walking. Be encouraged my friend, this journey will take you on a path to healing and freedom. Hang in there.

While our experiences may be different, the road to healing is the same in that we must face the truth of who we are and take responsibility for our actions and choices. Our healing comes from the truth. My friend, if you feel as though something is missing and that there must be more; I encourage you to keep reading. Where you are now will not be where you end up.

I was a successful emergency room nurse with two beautiful kids, a beautiful home and all the trappings of success. I was the proverbial corporate climber and had the experience, drive and knowledge to do it. I had it all. So, when my journey began with a painfully humbling realization that my life was not as 'perfect' as I thought, the house of cards came crashing down.

I was discontent with my career, so I switched jobs. I was unhappy in my marriage, so I filled my time with friends and parties. I was afraid of my emotions, so I escaped my reality by binging on food, drink, exercise and relationships. Yes indeed, I took the wrong path and ended up in a deep pit. Everything I thought to be truth was a lie. But in that darkness I learned to see. There is a saying, "I was blind and now I see. I was lost but now I am found." This became my truth. My eyes were opened the day I died.

My life didn't unravel over a course of a couple of months, though I would like to have thought that was the case. I learned it was a series of negative patterns and choices that got worse over the years.

There I was alone, crying in my room because I saw absolutely no possible way out. I couldn't tell anyone what was going on and I couldn't continue the insanity. I couldn't breathe I was crying so hard; I was completely at the end of my life and it could not continue. The guilt, the shame, the embarrassment I would feel when they learned my secrets. Have you ever been to that place where your spirit has finally died and there is nothing left? If you are there, now you have two choices, fall and die or jump and fly. I encourage you to jump and fly with me.

When I started this journey, my marriage was over, but by the grace and mercy of God, it was not only saved, it was healed! It is my prayer that you will find hope through my story and be encouraged to walk out your own journey of healing.

As I mentioned in my introduction, this journey will require you to work. It will require you to be brutally honest with yourself as you face your shortcomings, as well as your strengths. It will require you to journal the good, bad and indifferent. It will stretch you. It is important to remember that your journey won't have an end date as you will always be learning about yourself, growing and evolving to achieve your God-given purpose. Don't despair… it won't always be this difficult or daunting.

As for me, while my journey began many years ago, I remember it like it was yesterday. I remember just wanting to be "normal."

What exactly is normal? I couldn't tell you what it was then and I certainly can't describe it now. It just seemed like a good goal. We are unique and at the same time so predictable. Our emotional and spiritual stability seems to vary day to day, based on circumstances and happenstance. But it doesn't need to be this way. We can and should be in a place of peace regardless of the day-to-day struggles and drama.

This is why, wherever we are, it is important that our personal journey is exactly that, our own. No one can tell us what decisions to make or what is best for us. What works for one person is not always what works for another. Some people enjoy crowds while others like to be alone. Some folks need quiet to work while others need a radio playing in the background. Some may have trouble eating healthy but love to exercise while others may control every morsel that passes their lips, but hate the thought of breaking a sweat.

It is important to be open to change while understanding how we operate. We need to remember that we are the best qualified to make our own decisions.

Now, while I say, "We are best qualified to make our own decisions," I am reminded that I didn't quite see it that way when I was younger. In fact, it was easier to let others make decisions for me. I didn't have to take responsibility for the outcome. What I learned was that I often went along with things that I didn't want, and sadly suffered the consequences of those choices. I was furious at myself for allowing this to happen, but at the same time, I was grateful for the awareness. I could finally take responsibility for not taking responsibility. Ouch!

I gained a lot of insight about myself. In my business life, I was confident, self-assured and bold. In my personal life, I was insecure, unsure and always searching. I was a people pleaser who stuffed anger, resentment, bitterness, pain and un-forgiveness so deep down into my soul that it ended up poisoning me.

Rather than engage in conflict, I would lash out at myself with negative self-talk and give up my power. These negative tapes were my comfort. I didn't know how to give them up and quite frankly, it was as natural as breathing. Rather than doubt my decisions, I let others make them for me. It was difficult facing this truth about me. However, part of healing is being honest. I was required to dig deep and find out where those lies came from.

ENCOURAGEMENT

My friend, I urge you to first dig deep and get in touch, without judgment, with who you are. Get in touch not only with your own inner voice but with the voice of your Creator, God.

> *Psalm 32:8 "I will instruct you and teach you in the way you should go. I will counsel you and watch over you."*

Working together with Him will provide a way. It will provide absolute truth and it will provide light.

DEFINING YOUR FAITH

To start: Respond to each question as honestly as you can.

1. Who is God to me?
2. What is my relationship with God today?
3. Do I have doubts about who God is? If so, describe.

Congrats!!! You just started connecting your spirit to God.

The Christian faith believes that God exists in a triune, three in one. God the Father, He is our Creator who always was and always will be; His Son, Jesus Christ, died for our sins, and rose again, so that we could receive forgiveness and have a personal relationship with God. In John 14 Jesus promised that when He left, He would ask the Father to send a Spirit as our comforter and guide. This Holy Spirit dwells in us who love Christ and love the Father. This Holy trinity is the ultimate and total expression of God's love for us. As my friend Dave Bowerman, author of Higher Pursuits put it – "He has given us everything by giving all of Himself: His concern for us as Father, His involvement with us as Son, and His promptings in us as Spirit. For us, with us, and in us- He's held nothing back."

While the trinity is an expression of the love

God has for us, it is very clear we must accept this gift. It's important that we understand that God had to send Jesus to die for our sins. Jesus' death opened the door so that we could have a fully open, intimate real relationship with God. We are blind (and deaf) to this relationship until we open our hearts to that truth. Making this deliberate choice for yourself, pray "Father, I know I'm a sinner and I thank you for sending your Son. I accept the gift of forgiveness and grace. I want to walk with You. Open my eyes, open my ears to You. Help me to love You and trust You how You want me to."

Take a moment to thank God for wisdom, peace, comfort and strength. Thank Him for the gift of the Holy Spirit who will walk through this journey with you. I encourage you to find the answers with God's guidance. One of my favorite verses is *Jeremiah 29:11* *"For I know the plans I have for you." declares the Lord, "Plans to prosper you and not to harm you, plans to give you hope and a future."*

Take a moment to think about this verse and what your life is like right now. Does it bring you hope? What do you have surrounding this?

Do you think there is anything in your life right now that stops you from embracing these plans? If so, take a moment to name them honestly and boldly. Some examples may be substance abuse, anger, mistrust, gossip, unmanageable behaviors or thoughts.

The Bible is what God uses to teach us. In *2 Timothy 3:16* it reads *"All Scripture is God- breathed and is useful for teaching, rebuking, correcting and training in righteousness."* Learn about and trust what God says. You cannot control outcomes, you cannot force others to be who they are not and you have not been given authority to judge. We each have our own journey, our own struggles to overcome. Overcoming our own struggles grows us to be who we were meant to be – a unique, beautiful expression of love. So we are best suited to simply be a student of His word.

Write a short paragraph of what your life, if lived authentically in line with God, and without these barriers or strongholds, would look like. Don't be afraid to get creative, embrace true peace and freedom. What does it look like?

What does it mean to you to be spiritually healthy?

Where do your strengths lie and where do you need the most help?

APPLICATION

I consider myself an athlete. Sadly, I let work, family and life choke the time from physical fitness. However, I quickly realized that getting my life back on track meant doing it emotionally, spiritually and physically. Doing so gave me an opportunity to bring back my one love; mountain biking. I know... Florida's idea of a mountain is a bridge, but I would settle for the trails. There is nothing like riding the trails. You really have to pay attention every moment for there is no time for mind wandering or too much thinking. This was perfect as a healthy break from work, family and all the growth I was experiencing. It turned out to be like a very active meditation – just what my body and mind needed.

I quickly fell in love with the fast pace, sudden turns and obstacles, and the overall feeling of adventure and uncontrollable control. At first this new terrain was intimidating. I often had to stop at the obstacles and walk over them in order to be safe. But, after some practice, I just went for it. It wasn't long before I got stronger and looked forward to getting back in shape.

The stronger I grew, the more the adventure unfolded. This experience is very similar to my emotional and spiritual healing journey – intimidating and challenging while being invigorating and freeing.

That same unfolding is available to you!

 The Power of Change

Many years ago, I attended Al Anon at the recommendation of a friend – apparently my coping mechanisms were similar to that of a child of an alcoholic – even though no one in my sphere of influence was an alcoholic. That aside, I went to the meetings and gleaned some very helpful tips from the recovery principles, but never did what was necessary to change my habits and patterns.

So, while I learned the tools necessary to change my course, I continued to walk in denial in certain areas of my life. I never really embraced the fact that I had (have) the power to change.

What I learned is that healing is a process. It is a lifestyle. It takes commitment. Some days are better than others. And, most importantly, recovery looks different for each individual. While I might have an issue facing my shortcomings, someone else may have an issue letting go of control. It's important to understand and accept the fact that only you have the power to change you. Don't compare your journey with someone else.

As you begin this journey, I encourage you to embrace the truth. The truth about who you are today. What behaviors or habits have you grasped onto that really aren't serving a positive purpose for you? You will not be able to change if you don't face the things that need to be changed.

I encourage you to stick to the facts and stay grounded in the truth. *Yes, I say encourage often because it is important.* It is not always easy to face our own shortcomings. The truth about who we are and how we live and reality are often sugar coated by years or decades of denial. Denial is a coping mechanism that some of us may use. While it can be useful for a short period of time, it can also enable us.

DENIAL

Those of us working in critical areas see the benefit of when we tell a patient or family very bad news. There is almost a sense that they are not getting all of it all at once. With the news about the sudden death of my father, I remember feeling like something bad was coming, but the full force did not hit immediately. While denial enables us to handle the painful experiences, it also prohibits us from changing. If left unchecked it will slowly poison every area of our lives. Sometimes we can stay in that warm, safe denial phase – whether it is about a tragic event or the fact that you have a drinking problem. I will say it again, it's not easy to face our shortcomings, but it is imperative.

We are able to change when we take responsibility for our circumstances. Taking full ownership empowers us to face the strongholds and behaviors that hold us back. Once we recognize this, our strongholds begin to lose their power and we can begin living in freedom.

The power to change came to me when I reflected on some events that caused intense pain, regret, self-pity and unworthiness in me. As a nurse, I am committed to caring for people, it's what I do. So, when my dad had his first heart attack, he went through the cardiac rehab program I ran. He completed it successfully. Did I feel like I saved my dad? No. I wouldn't say I saved him, but I was an active part of his recovery. The sense of responsibility was raw. He did well, and I relaxed.

A couple of years later, my father had a massive heart attack and ended up back in "my" emergency room. This time he didn't survive. I remember when they told me, my mom and sisters were crying. I sat there thinking what I should do next; surely there was something I had to do. We needed to make phone calls, make plans. I remember thinking "I feel like this isn't so bad. It's sad to watch everyone be so sad, but I'm fine" This denial lasted a couple days. Then when it hit, I was angry.

How could I save so many other heart attack victims and not my dad? How could I let him die? He was so young and healthy. I felt so responsible for his death, but I never told anyone. I kept all the feelings in. There were too many to even filter through. I felt so worthless.

I couldn't handle the reality of the situation so I hid in work and stayed in denial for longer periods of time. It was easier. My escape mechanisms came in the way of working four jobs while raising two small children.

I found other places to hide. I stepped it up in the party scene, flirted more often and found other ways to feel worthy and "good about myself." When it didn't work, I refused to admit it, so I tried harder. I wouldn't look myself in the eye when I stood in front of the mirror. I just wanted to keep masking the problem and push myself farther into this fun, new distraction.

I was living a double life. On one side, I threw myself into church and learning about God, while at the same time walking in the world. At times I wanted to change, but the thought of what it would take was overwhelming. I didn't like what my life would look like without my coping mechanisms; frankly, it seemed boring.

Thank goodness my husband was not perfect, and I could blame him for many wrongs in our life. I prayed for my husband, "If only God would change him, life would be okay." I desperately wanted my husband to run to God. I thought that would make us a "healthy" family. Sadly, I learned that I could go to church and read the Bible eight hours a day, but if I didn't let it into my heart, I would never change.

The more I blamed Tom and prayed for him to get better, the worse I got. Neither of us embraced what it meant to be in relationship with God. While I heard that Jesus died for my sins, I didn't get what that meant for me. I was blind to my own "junk." I wasn't able to see things in reality and truth. The idea of changing was too much work so I stayed in denial about my own behavior.

It was so difficult at that time. I remember going to church aching to be like everyone else, aching to be good, wanting to be normal and praying for something better. While I couldn't quite see it, deep down I knew there was something better for me and my family. Even in the pit of depression, I knew life could get better. In hindsight, I credit my hope to God. In spite of my messy life, He loved me, He kept whispering hope and peace into my Spirit. That is the only explanation I have. Where else could the hope have come from?

Your race, religion, gender and/or financial status doesn't matter when it comes to life's problems. Eventually we will all come to a place where our lives are "unmanageable" in our eyes. It is how we respond to our daily situations that matter. We can choose to change or sit in dysfunction. It is our choice. Either way, we will always come up against a situation that will have the potential to make us or break us.

If you want to make it, then you have to face it head on. Accept the reality and honestly own up to anything that you may have caused. Once I could admit that I was miserable and didn't know what to do, there was progress. Once I realized I could list my husband's shortcomings easier and quicker than my own, there was progress.

Once I stopped beating myself up and admitted all of my self-defeating behaviors, there was progress. There was progress, but it wasn't over. My friend explained it like this "Once you finally wake up and realize you are lost in the forest, you still need to find your way out." That's exactly what it felt like.

The dysfunctional patterns are coping mechanisms that allow us to survive. So, in essence they work, but only for a while. Eventually, we have to face the pain in our lives; unmet expectations, failed relationships, poor choices, etc.

A woman helping me explained it best, "You were drowning and grabbed onto a log with both hands; it saved you. Now it's time to let go of the log. It's about to go over a waterfall and you need to let go and step onto dry land." It's hard to release what worked when you know the pain of reality that awaits you.

APPLICATION

Proverbs 3:5 "Lean on, trust in, and be confident in the Lord with all your heart and mind and do not rely on your own insight or understanding."

Can God count you righteous even if you are still carrying around addictions or unmanageable behaviors? Can He still love you if you are not free from strongholds? (Hint, the answer is a resounding yes to both questions)

1. What are some ways you use denial in your life?
2. Is there something in your life that you think is "not so bad" but you don't want anyone to know about it, or your loved ones are concerned?
3. On a scale of 1–10, how much faith do you have?

4. How do you know God is concerned with your day-to-day life?

5. What happens when your emotions cloud your judgment?

6. When do you give in to "victim thinking"? Victim thinking is when we blame our behavior on someone else. It's when we give up taking responsibility for our actions to someone or something else.

7. How are others responsible for how you feel sometimes?

8. Look again at what is stopping you from the plans God has for you. What holds you back these days? If you are honest and not in denial, you have plenty, everyone does. Choose one or two YOU would like to refer to and work on each time we are discussing these. This can be anything from gossiping at work to closet binge drinking. This is not meant in any way to make you feel guilt or shame. This exercise is to open us up to the growth God wants to have. What is the one thing really sabotaging me right now? Opening our eyes with God is safe. He will show you the areas to grow as you are ready to see them.

As you move along this journey, you will learn to become more responsible for your emotional, physical, spiritual and psychological well-being. Your circumstances, no matter what they are, are yours to own. If we are helpless victims, then there is nothing we can do about it and that is simply unacceptable. Every time we want to blame someone else for a circumstance, we are wasting time.

My friend, I encourage you to get real with yourself and take the time to identify your role in the situation. There is no stopping the progress you can make if you simply face the truth and have the willingness to change. Remember, feelings are not facts.

One of the things God showed me, is still showing me, is a lack of self discipline in the area of food. I know through experience that if I eat too much chocolate, I get sick. I can't have a couple of M&M's because it awakens a monster inside me. Besides, what kind of freak eats a couple of M&M's anyway? *(Sorry, I went off track for a minute but I'm just saying, if you can eat a handful of M&M's and walk away maybe YOU need help, just a thought.)*

Ok, back to my point. Sadly, it has been an all or nothing battle with chocolate. There is no in between. God is teaching me that my truth requires me to avoid chocolate while I learn and practice self-discipline. Perhaps someone who struggles with alcohol can understand my struggle with food. The patterns of addiction are so similar it's uncanny. Over indulge (sounds better than binge) and then wallow in guilt, repeat, repeat, repeat. Insane – right? There was nothing I could do to stop myself, until I accepted that I didn't have the power to change without giving it up to my God.

Chocolate, anger, control, gambling, alcohol, perfectionism and (add your examples); this list is inexhaustible. It doesn't matter what strongholds we have; however it does matter how we handle them. If you want freedom, you will have to surrender to God and His ways. It is through surrendering that you will find the power to make your own choices and the power to change.

Once I began to understand what it meant to surrender to God, I was able to embrace the hard truth of what it would take to change. I learned all about boundaries, control and codependence. I understood that my perfectionism was an escape mechanism and not an expectation from God. I began to live with the idea that God loved me exactly the way I was and He was going to use my challenges to raise me. Walking with this sense of acceptance and openness to guidance was refreshing and became very comfortable. Comfort, for me, brought forth serenity and even more awareness.

> *2 Timothy 3:16–17 "All scripture is God breathed and is used for teaching, rebuking, correcting and training in righteousness, so that the man of God may be thoroughly equipped for every good work."*

SELF EXAMINATION

1. Can you begin a relationship with God if you give into emotion and can't get a handle on your life?
2. Choose three different themes important to you now and look up what the Bible has to say about it. For example – one of the first things I felt I wanted to understand was temptation.

Why did it feel like when I gave into a little, it turned into a lot? I was pleasantly surprised at what I found and how the answers were so relevant to my situation. I frequently prayed "lead me not into temptation" but then still found myself not only tempted, but giving in.

Matthew 4:3-10 teaches that Jesus was tempted and how He resisted temptation. He quoted scripture, He used what His father gave him and it worked.

In Galatians 6:1 it explains that even when we feel strong but we are going to help someone else, we should not go alone "Lest we be tempted".

Okay, so I was starting to realize, maybe I'm more normal

than I think. If it was in the bible it was important to God. If Jesus had to go through it, it must be okay that I'm going through it. If God found this important enough that I could find this topic easily enough and in a few places, it validated I was on the right path.

The real answer to my utter excitement was in James1 12-15. This was the answer I needed! This was exactly what was happening to me, how could this be? My own earthly desires entice and draw me away. If I feed that, it grows, and when sin is full grown it kills me. So for me, this meant to watch out for that little monster that peaks her head out. She speaks in my own voice and tells me how much fun it will be, or good it will feel or anything else that I find attractive. When I give in to her, my spirit suffers. After learning this and really digesting this, I can see the temptation for the lie that it is. That is what I need to resist and ignore. I do not feed her or encourage her because when I do, it becomes unquenchable and I get lost.

It is better if I see the lie for what it is and then ask myself, "What is it that I really need?" Why is this temptation so attractive to me? What's missing? Usually I've learned I need a break, I need some time in nature, I need some quiet time with God to speak to my soul, I need a nap, I need to laugh or any number of other health sustaining activities that lift me up instead of take me down.

See if any of these help…

When you find yourself feeling anxious, look up Philippians 4:6. Depressed? Proverbs 12:25. The Good Book is filled with comfort when you are afraid. Try Luke 12:32 and 2 Timothy1:7.

There is so much in the Bible that will speak to your individual spirit when you open your heart and open the book. If you don't find what you are looking for, I promise you will find what you need. God is funny that way. I wonder if it amuses him when we think we know what is best for ourselves. I wonder how much he enjoys filling our hearts with exactly what we need, but in a totally unexpected way.

I can't help but get the clear sense that He is okay with me struggling with life and it can take however long it's going to take. But I also get a clear sense that He loves giving me more than I've asked for, especially when I leave it all up to Him. Lastly, I also feel like He enjoys my faith. I think this is why He loves to come through at the very last moment. It's almost like He is sitting in heaven, smiling, saying "What? I totally had that. Were you starting to worry?"

ENCOURAGEMENT

My friend, this journey is going to be difficult. I encourage you to release your feelings and trust God to walk you through it. When I would come upon those little wooden bridges while trail riding, I would become completely stressed out. My mind would go straight to the negative. I would picture myself riding off the side or how much it would hurt if I did fall off.

When I'd reach the bridge I would become afraid, almost panic and then I would jump off my bike, run over the bridge and hop back on. One day we hit a bridge that was very low sitting and not quite as intimidating.

Don't get me wrong – I still was afraid but I decided to try. I purposely chose healthy thoughts and did what I knew to be right. I kept my eyes on where I was heading, not down. I relaxed my shoulders and forearms so my steering wouldn't waver back and forth. I focused my thoughts on the strong steady push and pull, and kept a steady circle with my legs. I took back my responsibility of how I was thinking and it worked.

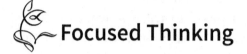# Focused Thinking

2 Corinthians 10:5 (NIV) "We demolish arguments and every pretension that sets itself up against the knowledge of God, and we take captive every thought to make it obedient to Christ."

Friend, be encouraged. You are on a path of growth. You are courageous. You are strong. You are loved. You are bold. And, most of all you are able. You are able to face your pain, your past and your part. Dig in. Don't give up or give in. Trust the process. Trust God.

The day I heard "Woman, why do you cry?" was the day my life changed forever. I was scared. I was embarrassed. I was fearful. In my eyes I only saw darkness. In my thoughts, I saw a lonely broken woman in a broken marriage. But, I was not alone. My God showed up. In fact, He held me close. He spoke to me and comforted me. In my brokenness, He gave me hope. When it seemed the darkest, He gave me a sliver of light – just a sliver, but it broke through the darkness.

This was when my relationship with Jesus shifted from awareness to personal.

When I first embarked on my journey, fear consumed me. I allowed my thoughts to run rampant, which subsequently led to uncontrollable emotions. I was a mess and I was confused because "things" weren't getting better. It wasn't until I read and received 2 Corinthians 10:5 that I finally understood the power of my thoughts and how they controlled my reactions and responses.

Once I began to pay attention to my thought patterns, I began to recognize how I fed them with fear.

I am sure that I don't have to tell you about the fearful thoughts that bombarded me when I embarked on my healing journey. They are likely all too familiar to you. The fear of being rejected, fear of being judged, fear of losing a job, fear of losing love, fear, fear and more fear. When I finally understood that I had power over fear by simply taking my thoughts captive, I diligently set out to protect my thought life. Was it easy? No. Was it worth it? Yes. Am I still practicing? Absolutely!

I learned that my thoughts ran rampant when I was emotionally charged up or exhausted. I had to diligently guard my thoughts while reminding myself that feelings and emotions aren't facts. This empowered me to take responsibility for my actions rather than react negatively or blame.

Have you ever responded to an email or text with venom and vengeance only to regret it the second you hit 'send'? Well, I have, more than once, and it was horribly embarrassing afterward. While I would like to say that I am completely healed from reacting hastily, I am proud to say that I am a work in progress.

Self-awareness takes practice and humility. I encourage you to take a moment of honest self-reflection.

- Did anything mentioned previously speak to you?
- Do you find yourself blaming everyone else rather than owning up to your part?
- Do you see your emotions as "out of control" at times? (Is there a certain person or people who bring out the worse in you? If so, write down their names

and solutions as to how you can limit your exposure while you are working on you.

- Of the behaviors you have identified that you want to work on, is there something that may seem too big to handle? Why?

While I loved walking out my journey with trusted friends, I was blessed to have a trusted professional who provided unbiased and honest feedback. I encourage you to seek a trained professional when you need it. It can be a difficult and painful journey. But, do not fear, it is worth every second... there is victory.

> *"Such love has no fear, because perfect love expels all fear. If we are afraid, it is for fear of punishment, and this shows that we have not fully experienced his perfect love."* 1 John 4:18(NLT)

There is a time and a season for all things. This is your season for healing. This is your season of self-care. It is time for you to guard your heart and thoughts. People may not want you to change; in fact, they may tell you that you don't need to change. You know why you are on this journey. Stay focused. Stay the course.

The day I began the twelve (slow) steps out of a dark hole, I chose to trust a God whom I hardly knew. I also found a counselor (a wonderful woman) who held me accountable as I dug up the roots of my strongholds. I quickly learned that freedom and maturity came with taking full responsibility for my actions, reactions and choices.

The spirit of hope was planted deep within my soul and it gave me a vision of a better life.

My dear sister, be encouraged. The fact is that you are able to change your life. You are empowered to receive healing, physically, emotionally and spiritually.

CAPTURING NEGATIVE THOUGHTS

"If they knew I did (fill in your secret), they won't like or respect me. They will think I am a bad (person, parent, wife, friend)."

These thoughts are wrapped up in shame and pride. If you dwell on them, you are likely to spiral into a pool of guilt and shame where you further feed a spirit of unworthiness. The darkness of an untold secret grows and eats away at our spirit. These thoughts of shame and guilt hold us back. We can't possibly move forward into a healthy and positive life when we feel unworthy of receiving that life.

Sister, it is time to let go of the guilt and shame. It is time for you to trust God and let Him walk you through the purging process. I encourage you to work through your strongholds, regrets and offenses against others. Use the chart on the following page.

It may seem daunting. No, it is daunting. It is difficult. If it were easy everyone would be doing it. However, you are ready to dig in. You are ready to let go of the self-sabotaging thoughts and actions.

It is time you forgive yourself for your mistakes, poor choices and poor actions. It is time to ask God to forgive you and set you free from the burdens of your past. All you have to do is ask. Envision yourself being washed clean. God sent His only Son, Jesus Christ, to die for your sins.

You are forgiven. It doesn't matter if you don't "feel" forgiven. This will come with time and understanding. If you think you don't deserve it, welcome to the family, my friend. I too felt that way. *"For God so loved the world that He gave His one and only Son, that whoever believes in Him shall not perish but have eternal life." John 3:16*

Be encouraged. Things may not turn around quickly. Sometimes it takes time to accept the gift of what Jesus did on the cross for us. It is God's gift of mercy and grace that frees us. A gift we can't even wrap our brain around receiving. Trust the process.

NAME	THOUGHT BEHIND IT	REPENTANCE
Fear	I need to control the situation. What if things don't turn out right?	Lord help me to find your peace and trust you, even when I walk in the valley of the shadow of death.
Perfectionism	Mistakes are bad. People will judge me.	Lord help me to love myself the way you love me, kindly and gently. Help me focus only on pleasing you.
Guilt	I can't let go of past mistakes	Jesus help me to accept the gift of the cross. Open my mind and soften my heart to know your love and forgiveness.
Pride	My work is better than theirs	Humble me Father; keep me from thinking too much of myself. Remind me that all good things come from you and I'm nothing apart from you.
Feeling Inadequate	I am not _____ enough	God thank you that in my weakness you are strong.

I was told to receive God's grace and mercy. I didn't quite understand it until I heard my pastor explain it like this: Mercy is when we don't get what we deserve. Grace is when we get what we don't deserve.

Understand that taking personal responsibility for our part and confessing our wrongs make it easier to accept His mercy and His grace. It is what Jesus did on the cross that provides the mercy for our forgiveness. It is God's love that provides grace so we can enjoy our blessings and learn from our trials. So once you accept His forgiveness, there isn't much else you can do. He loves you, He forgives you and He wants you to be in Heaven with Him for eternity. It's not complicated or convoluted.

Romans 10: 9-10 "If you confess with your mouth that Jesus is Lord and believe in your heart that God raised Him from the dead, you will be saved."

- Jesus died for your sins. This was a gift. Do you accept this gift that He gave you to cleanse you of your sin?
- Can you sit quietly with God and admit what you think are your worst sins? Just confess them to Him and feel the lack of condemnation and feel His acceptance and love.
- He understands we need forgiveness. We can't get this right. We need Jesus – accept the gift and let it do its amazing work inside of you.

CONQUERING FEAR

The decision to change was the hardest for me. I was so afraid of failing. I was afraid of not being "able" to change. I was afraid of facing my pain. There is that dreaded feeling again. Fear can and does paralyze us.

A spirit of fear does not come from God. He gives us a spirit of peace, joy and faith. Unfortunately, it almost seems necessary for us to walk through the fear in order to grow. There is no way around it. Remember that your journey is unique and personal. We are not wrong for feeling fear; it tends to come when we move out of our comfort zone. However, the closer we walk in fellowship with God, the easier it becomes to recognize and rebuke fear. It also becomes easier to ignore the fear; you get more comfortable being uncomfortable. It is a discomfort that will have a sense of safety and trust.

When God put it on my heart to share my journey with other women, I was excited. God using my pain and experiences to set other women free from the captivity of hopelessness was a modern day example of His promise in Isaiah 61:3 "...bestow on them a crown of beauty for ashes, the oil of joy instead of mourning and a garment of praise instead of despair." I learned that by allowing God to use my pain for His glory, I was allowing Him to heal all of my wounds.

Now, don't get me wrong...it hasn't been an easy walk. Even though He told me to share my story I argued about the details. I was afraid if I put out my failures, struggles and strongholds I would be judged unfairly. The thought of co- workers gossiping behind my back, or someone judging my children because of my actions hit me deeply.

Were these things happening? I had no idea, but I let the spirit of fear plant those seeds. So, I resisted God in the area of complete truth. "Resisted" isn't actually accurate – It was more like an outright NO. It was more of a denial that He was leading me in that direction. At that time, progress came to a halt. I was given time to realize the benefit to the people I would help was greater than the vulnerability that would come with actually publishing this.

The facts are that God saved a marriage even after divorce papers were drawn up and unbearable pain had been inflicted. God saved my entire family, He saved our finances and most importantly, He saved me from me. But after all of that, I still argued with Him about the depth and details of my experience that He called me to share. Well, if you can't tell by now, I finally submitted to God and did what He called me to do. I shared my experience as a broken person. My fears and struggles are for Him to use. I trust Him to guard the hearts and minds of my loved ones. He has never let me down and He won't start now.

I feel it's important to remind you that God would love me just as much if I chose to write nothing. It is my growth and my path that would change. What He has for me is beyond anything I can imagine. I pray every day for Him to use me.

I'm fully aware it gets uncomfortable, but it's worth it to me. On August 28th I only wanted three things: for God to keep my children healthy and safe; teach me how to live a life of integrity; and let the divorce not be ugly for them.

I've received exponentially more than I imagined all to the glory of God. I have a healthy marriage. He gave me a new life of abundance. Both of our children are healthy, independent adults. I have a successful, rewarding career and I am blessed enough to give away what He has given me. I owe Him everything. It's all His and I wouldn't have it any other way.

I hope you are as excited as I am right now! Imagine the possibilities and adventures He has awaiting you.

Take a moment and ask Him for the faith you need to face your fears. It isn't going to be easy, but He will give you all that you need. God is never early and He is never late. Trust Him. I encourage you to read His word and receive your strength in Him. You are strong and courageous. *"Have I not commanded you? Be strong and of good courage; do not be afraid, nor be dismayed, for the Lord your God is with you wherever you go." Joshua 1:9*

What a beautiful message. Sit with the comfort of knowing that God has chosen you to be His daughter. He knows your struggles. He knows you need Him and He is with you wherever you go. Sit comfortably in this truth.

- What fears do you have that keep you from completely handing it all over to God?

Even Jesus experienced weakness and asked God to take away the trial (before He was led to His death.) In Luke 22:42-43 He cried out *"Father, if it is your will, take this cup away from Me: nevertheless not My will, but Yours, be done."* Then an angel appeared to Him from Heaven, strengthening Him.

- What does it feel like when you have to do something you don't want to do?
- What does it feel like to be terrified to move forward?
- What did Jesus do when He was terrified?

Psalm 27:1 "The Lord is my light and my salvation; whom shall I fear? The Lord is the strength of my life; of whom shall I be afraid?"

- What fears do you have today that you have not brought to your loving Father?
- What are real fears and what are lies that the devil may try to use against you?

2 Timothy 1:7 "For God has not given us a spirit of fear, but of power and of love and of a sound mind." (Some interpretations say self-discipline).

What does it look like today to feel the fear, acknowledge it and move forward anyway? Meditate on that. What would you do? What would you change?

Describe in detail what your life would be like if fear did not hold you back. What accomplishments would occur? Where would you live? What would your family be like? What would you look like?

Challenge yourself. What would it look like if you walked through the fear – got out the other side? Can you envision yourself incredibly successful? Can you feel and see that accomplishment?

APPLICATION

I often find similarities between my habits and struggles in my healing journey with my habits and struggles in my physical journey. While trail biking one day, I noticed that I kept getting off my bike when the path seemed a little too steep or the roots seemed too big and complex to navigate without getting hurt. Not only was it slowing me down to keep getting off of my bike to go over the roots or up a hill, it was inhibiting my ability to increase my skill.

There simply was no way to get better without conquering the fear of not getting up the hill or falling on the roots.

As I walked over the roots, I saw that they weren't nearly as terrible as I thought.

The next time I came to a difficult obstacle, I trusted the power of my legs to propel me over it. I focused on the task at hand. I didn't look too far ahead. I knew I had what I needed at that moment to conquer the obstacle right in front of me. Some obstacles are more difficult than others, but I trust myself enough that I could push through it. And, that is what it has been like on my healing journey. In the moments with the greatest fear, I dug in and trusted God to get me through the difficult parts and guess what? He did.

 **The Power Of Love**

Zephaniah 3:17 "The Lord your God is with you, He is mighty to save. He will take great delight in you and He will quiet you with His love, He will rejoice over you with singing."

The word love is tossed about with such carelessness that I wonder if it has lost its true meaning. I love horses, I love this weather, I love my bike, and so on. But love, real love is deep and abiding. Real love moves beyond circumstance and feeling.

- What comes to mind when you hear the word love?
- Is it a noun or a verb? Is it a feeling?
- Is it dependent on any circumstances or outside influence?

I challenge you to begin thinking of love as a verb. I encourage you to think of loving people with your thoughts, prayers, actions, words, and behaviors. Stay with me here because I'm also going to ask you to love no matter how you are feeling (ouch). It is no easy task. In fact, it can be tough to do.

I found it easier to love others once I was able to truly love and accept myself. Of course, that too was a process, and it wasn't until I began to believe what God said about me that I was able to accept and love myself in spite of my past painful choices.

Have you chosen to believe His word about you and about

your life today? If you are struggling in your faith and trust in God, please understand there is no condemnation in Christ Jesus. You are not inadequate. In fact, you are at the right place at the right time. Developing your walk and relationship with God takes time, just as your physical relationships take time.

Trust the process. Healing from old habits, hurts and mistakes takes forgiveness, intention and time. Be patient with yourself as you grow in self-awareness. Some days you will take one step forward and two steps back. Do your best to forgive yourself when you have a set-back. It's okay.

As God gives you grace and mercy, you must give yourself grace and mercy. I know it is easy to pick out the failures. Focusing on the mistakes, failures and sin will take you down. Someone once asked me why, after what Jesus did for me, I still felt guilt and shame. I said I felt like the forgiveness was for everyone else. She lovingly (sort of) told me that I was facing Jesus and telling Him that what He did on the cross was not good enough. Stop. Don't beat yourself up.

This is your journey to healing. It won't always be easy and it won't always be difficult. There will be days where you will second guess everything you say; you will question your motives; and distrust your own actions, it's alright. Don't try too hard. Simply pay attention and recognize that the lesson might be a victory. Everything will happen in God's time. It's progress, not perfection. What's important is what He wants, and He wants you to do life with Him.

TRUSTING GOD

When I began my journey, I didn't really know God. I knew there was a God. I accepted Jesus Christ as my Savior, but I didn't know of His awesome love, forgiveness, peace, mercy and grace.

As I learned to trust God, I became willing to let go of false beliefs embedded in me as a child. Sister, I want you to know that He is acutely aware of you; He is loving, kind and mighty powerful. He is waiting for you to get to know Him and the great plans He has for you.

In order for you to truly know Him, you must first choose Him of your own free will. He will show you His truth. It is time to ignore what society and the "new-age" teaching says about you. Once you know the truth of God, it is so much easier to do the right thing.

Your relationship with God is yours. I encourage you to rest in His presence and allow Him to pour out His love on you today. It doesn't matter where you are, how you feel or what people say about you. God loves you and wants you to be at peace. Once you allow Him to love and minister to your spirit, you will be able to start loving yourself and others just as He commands.

Take a moment. Meditate on this scripture: *"God showed how much He loved us by sending His one and only Son into the world so that we might have eternal life through Him. This is real love—not that we loved God, but that He loved us and sent His Son as a sacrifice to take away our sins." 1 John 4:9-10*

Yes, He loves you! He loves you, my sweet sister. He loves you right where you are. There is no need to clean yourself up. If you were the only person on this earth, He would have still sent His son to die for your sins. He would still be calling your name. Beloved, He doesn't want you to sit in your pain. He wants to see you set free, but you have to be willing to let it go. You have to do the work. Trust Him to strengthen you.

Allow God to move you from the darkness of false beliefs and into the truth. *"When the spirit of truth comes, he will guide you into all truth." John 16:13*

Sit quietly with this statement for a couple minutes. Just be in

God's presence. Let Him quiet you with His love. Get comfortable with being uncomfortable. There is no judgment here, just openness to His presence.

SAVED FROM DIVORCE

When Tom and I first separated, I would have told you that I still loved him as a person but I had fallen out of love with him. I've heard other women say this before and even now it sounds ridiculous. At that time, I was looking at love as the feelings I had while we were courting; you know, the warm fuzzy excitement that is present in the first six months of all relationships. I soon learned that's not love. That's infatuation. Love is acceptance. Love is willingness to serve without expecting anything in return. Love is understanding that the relationship is sometimes 50/50, 90/10, 100/10. In the beginning of my (our) journey to healing, Tom and I had caused each other so much pain, we easily could have justified divorce.

In fact, when we first separated, some friends encouraged me to get the divorce over with as quickly as possible and often reaffirmed my belief that nothing would change. Some encouraged me to "get out and start dating" and tried to comfort me by telling me that more than half of my kids' friends had divorced parents. It was tempting to get it over with quickly. To be honest, I was tired of trying. I remember looking through the Bible seeking scripture that would justify divorce. While I was looking for justification, God was pouring into me. He was teaching me how to be a better wife, mother and friend.

That is our awesome God. He didn't beat me over the head or condemn me for trying to divorce. He gently led me to restoration. He taught me to forgive and accept forgiveness; to be honest with myself about everything; and to love myself. Once I reached out for God, He scooped me up and took me on the adventure of a lifetime.

Although we remained separated for three years, we were never able to finalize the divorce. We took the time to get healthy, doing exactly what we needed to move forward. I am so thankful that we both found our own unique and intimate relationship with God. Through our relationship with God, we found a way to combat our own strongholds and society's view of marriage. We quickly learned that the only way to be in a mature, healthy relationship is to be a mature, healthy individual.

LOVE IS A VERB

As I navigated the land of separation and co- parenting, I had a choice to be bitter and angry or to be kind and forgiving. In the beginning, we didn't like each other very much, but we did our best to honor our children by working together to ensure their best interests were at heart. I made sure that he had plenty of time with the children and I did my best to help them move through the struggles of bouncing between two homes. He made it a point to ask about my well-being and made sure he provided for our needs.

In our hearts, we believed the marriage was over, but we agreed that co-parenting our children required us to be friends. We were able to honor each other and operate out of love because of our relationship with God. Naturally, without God, we would have been bitter, resentful and angry.

Don't get me wrong, this didn't happen overnight. It was a process. It took time. At first it was awkward and sometimes not very genuine. Eventually, the positive attitudes produced positive results. After awhile people said that we got along better separated than most people who were married. In hindsight, I am glad that other people (including our children) saw the change in us before we did.

Love, – the action – not the feeling is what changed everything and still does today. We are not going to feel lovingly towards each other all the time. The difference is, no matter what the feeling, our behavior loves.

Even today, if we are not getting along and the feelings of frustration peak and emotions are running high my husband will look at me and say, "Let's pray."

It infuriates me and I just want to scream. Not because I don't want him to pray, but because he is right and at that moment I am way too emotional to settle down to pray. It feels like the most unnatural thing to do, and I'm sure it's not going to make a difference. He takes my hands in his, while I close my eyes and turn away.

Sometimes I may even stomp my feet, but it does not stop him. He pushes forward and prays. The beautiful thing is that in spite of my pouting, the Holy Spirit moves in and softens my heart and brings healing to the situation – every time. [For the record, pouting is Tom's word, not mine. I don't pout!]

I am honored that my husband has become such a man of God. I love this man and I need him to be the leader God has called him to be just as he needs me to be the wife God called me to be. The wonderful thing is that his logical, unemotional behavior does not dictate my actions, just as my stubborn, chaotic, controlling, emotional issues have no bearing on his actions. We now have the marriage that God designed, and it goes against most of society's view of marriage.

We don't need to understand. We just need to know that God's view of marriage works.

IDENTIFYING YOUR PART

An important part of this journey is recognizing the real reason
you're annoyed with someone. I learned that when I was upset at
him for procrastinating, I was avoiding something. When I was upset
at him for not paying attention, I wasn't paying attention. When I
was upset at him for being too quick to anger, I was being overly
emotional.

God was teaching me to recognize my shortcomings. The
things that bothered me most about other people were the very
things I hated about myself.

*James 4: 7-8 "So humble yourselves before God. Resist the devil
and he will flee from you. Come close to God, and God will come
close to you."*

- What behaviors do you see in others that really get
  you frustrated?
- In all honesty, what about those behaviors do you see
  in yourself?
- What are some ways we minimize our behavior so it
  doesn't seem "so bad"?
- It is time to name your behaviors and address them
  boldly and confidently.
- What do you do to "make you feel better" that you
  wish you didn't?
- Is it holding you back or making it worse?
- Are you being completely honest with yourself and God?

*Romans 8:28 "And we know that all things work together for
good to those who love God, to those who are called according to
His purpose."*

- What ways could God use your struggles for His good?
- Think of someone who has come through a difficult trial and used it to bring hope to others.
- Do you think they were afraid to step out?
- How do you think they were able to do it? Sister, be encouraged. While some days are more difficult than others, understand that you are doing better than you are feeling. Feeling better is simply a frame of mind. Happiness is frequently based on circumstances. Joy is built on hope and faith. I found joy. You will find joy.

ENCOURAGEMENT

On your journey you will learn many lessons. And, they will come from different places. While trail riding, I am reminded to keep my eye on the path because every now and then a tree will "come out of nowhere" and knock me on my face. I glance down or back for a second (rookie mistake) and bam! I know I'm not supposed to look away. I know the scenery can change in a second, but sometimes I just can't help it. I lose focus and look away from my path. Inevitably, I end up on my face and a little bruised, but I get up, brush myself off, hop on my bike and get back on the trail. Lesson learned, (again).

This happens in recovery. If you find yourself looking back at your past, you might just end up getting knocked off your path. Don't beat yourself up. Brush it off and move forward. There will be setbacks, but you will learn to recognize them just as I recognized the importance of looking at the path in front of my tires – not behind me and not too far ahead.

Healthy Relationships

Ecclesiastes 4:10-12 says, "For if either of them falls, the one will lift up his companion. But woe to the one who falls when there is not another to lift him up. Furthermore, if two lie down together they keep warm, but how can one be warm alone? And if one can overpower him who is alone, two can resist him. A cord of three strands is not quickly torn apart."

Do other people's actions or words cause you to feel or behave in a certain way? Do you feel as though your negative reactions are automatic? Do you desire to have deeper relationships with less conflict? If you answered, "Yes" to any of these questions, take heart... you are on the right path.

Our relationships are important to God. He longs for us to abide in healthy, selfless relationships. He longs for us to let go of our idea of what a "good" relationship is and to walk in what He created as the perfect relationship. However, the only way to get there is to first have a relationship with the Lord. As with all relationships, it takes time and practice.

I encourage you to take the time to sit in the presence of God. I encourage you to find a quiet place to breathe slowly and relax in His presence. He longs for you to talk to Him about whatever is on your mind; good, bad, happy, sad, easy, ugly, dirty, mean, whatever. Bring it to the One you can trust completely.

Relax. He knows your mind will wander, your phone will ring or someone will interrupt, but be persistent and simply do the best you can. He will not waver or change; He does not become tired or annoyed. You are in a relationship; you just spoke to Him – now listen. He calls you to trust Him and Him alone, completely. Allow Him to unveil truths to you when you are ready to see them.

He longs for you to draw near to Him. As you learn to trust Him and sit in His presence, you begin to learn selflessness. You will learn to leave your agenda and expectations at the door. Imagine if you went into your relationships with family, friends and business associates without an agenda or expectations. Do you think they would be more harmonious?

One of the most beautiful things that I have learned on this journey is that my relationship with God, our Creator, never stops growing. It is constantly evolving and expanding into areas I couldn't possibly foresee. As I eagerly look to the next thing to work on, God reminds me that He is in charge of my growth and it is all in His timing. I am thankful for this because some of the pain I've faced was intense. I am glad He lets me up for air and I'm able to see the growth for what it is.

During a particularly difficult period in our separation, I had conflicting emotions and life was confusing. I found myself desperate to escape and avoid life. While it was a painful, lonely time, I grew. I grew to rely on Him more, as long as I didn't run away. I just learned to focus on the day. I simply kept doing what I needed to do that day, the best I could and trusted it would pass. I wasn't perfect, and my imperfection did not disappoint my Heavenly Father. I learned I could trust Him completely; even when my job was impossible and the people seemed like they were from another planet, He gave me peace.

As you begin to develop your one-on-one relationship with God, you will find that you desire Him more and more. Remain open to His presence, seek guidance throughout the day, stay aware, look for answers, and thank Him. Through your relationship with God, you will learn what a healthy relationship looks like.

Do your best to sit in God's presence and read His Holy Word on a daily basis. The more you read the Bible, the more you will see it as the love letter that it truly is. As you grow on this journey, you will begin to redefine what is important. When the Pharisees' asked Jesus what the most important law was to God, his response (I'm paraphrasing) was 'Worship the one true God and put no other gods above Him and secondly, love your neighbor as yourself.'

In the beginning, I had a difficult time under- standing why it was so important to be in fellowship with others. I am an introvert by nature. I am a nurse currently running a local emergency department. I am attentive to my loved ones well- being and enjoy being a servant of God. Yet, I reenergize by being alone. I crave silence. I'm not big on chit chat; and social events drain me. However, through obedience to God, I understand my boundaries better.

I am able to acknowledge and honor who I am exactly how God made me. I learned to love others, speak the truth and set healthy boundaries. I've learned what's important is what is in my heart. Do I want to be alone to escape or do I simply need a break and to care for myself.

When I get into situations where I'm tired, overwhelmed and overworked, the old me would have believed "I should enjoy this – don't be a downer" and gone full throttle until I was spent, but then slide into my self-destructive patterns to feel "better."

The new me can recognize my limits and empowers me to honor myself through rest, prayer, and restoration before expecting more from myself. Am I perfect at this? No, sometimes before I realize it I've agreed to more responsibility and committed to a few too many things and I have to step back. I regroup for a time and figure out where I took the wrong turn.

I always start in my heart. What is my heart saying? Am I feeling love and compassion, clarity of thought and confidence? Or am I frustrated, avoiding, annoyed and sarcastic? Love means providing hope, support and compassion. To love does not mean to give everything you have plus anything more you can muster. Love shouldn't drain us; it's meant to lift and fill us. I'm so grateful to have finally learned to love well.

SHORT COMINGS

We are called to minister to each other, care for each other and love each other. We are also called to let others learn from their own trials and have their own relationship with God. When we cross a boundary by trying to control or take ownership for someone else's feelings or behavior, we hijack their lesson.

We get in the way of God working in their lives. What motivates us to take over for God? Usually, it's our own selfishness. I know, it sounds harsh. It takes a long time and some practiced self-awareness sometimes before we can even identify this behavior. For the most part, we do this with a genuinely kind and giving heart. In fact, I would be the first one to tell you that I was the farthest thing from being selfish. I was a give, give, giver oh, even if you didn't ask for it, I would sacrificially give it. But, what was my motive?

As a mom, when I provide too much, do I love or am I desperately trying to remain needed? As kids get older, it's important for them to experience their own consequences. If, my son or daughter was 18 years old and I was still waking them for school and making lunches, then I'm not helping them. Actually, I'm blocking their growth and maturity.

Being a good mother is not constantly tending to every need, but making the right decision. Teenagers need to learn to wake up on their own and get to school; they need to figure it out. When they don't figure it out, natural consequences need to occur and they learn. Perhaps my need to remain needed is the actual problem in this situation.

God is working in all our lives. We each have unique journeys to travel; be aware when your focus moves off yourself and onto another – where are you going? Remember the obstacles God created for you to grow? Well, He does the same for others. So, before you reach out to "save" or "fix" someone, ask yourself if the trial is their opportunity for growth. Talk to God about it. There is this sense you will get, it's called being convicted, when God is trying to correct you. Look for that sense often, pay attention to it and act accordingly. It is not a feeling of shame or guilt; it is more like a realignment of sorts.

When the Holy Spirit convicts us of a behavior or action, it does not give us permission to convict or judge others if they are doing the same thing. That still small voice and correction is for our own journey; we are not to reflect it onto others. God alone judges; He alone knows our hearts and what led us to make the choices we made. It is our role to love others and respect their relationship with God if they choose to have one. This way they can learn for themselves of the grace of the One True God.

Ephesians 5:15-16 "So be careful how you live. Don't live like fools, but like those who are wise. Make the most of every opportunity in these evil days."

- What is your interpretation of this scripture? Does following Jesus seem boring?
- What is healthy, re-energizing fun for you?

- What has God given you for your enjoyment?

Deuteronomy 6:5 "You shall love the Lord your God with all your heart, with all your soul and with all your strength."

- How could we love and serve a God who has everything and needs nothing?

Always remember, we are all human and we are all created equal. No matter what caliber of person you are attracting, they will at some point disappoint you. Everyone messes up, but when people we love hurt us, it can be devastating.

When this happens it is imperative that we seek one-on-one time with our God. It is only when our heart is in communion with the Holy Spirit that we are able to discern the truth. When you have a significant disagreement with your spouse, for example, it is crucial not to draw everyone into the situation. It is crucial to be clear – is this a pattern of behavior that I regularly find myself in? Or, do I need to offer grace and forgiveness even when that seems impossible?

It's encouraging to spend time with people who can lift us up. It's healthy to have people in your life that do this. We must remember that no one, and I mean no one, is perfect. Just because I trust someone doesn't mean I expect them never to mess up. We have moments where we disappoint someone; we may say the wrong thing, do the wrong thing, buy the wrong thing, act the wrong way. You get the point. Also, we can get disappointed by others by having unrealistic expectations.

Remember God is only interested in the condition of your heart. Every situation is unique and it is in our own best interest to forgive quickly. It is okay to get out of an abusive, dysfunctional relationship; it's not okay to run just because things get tough.

When things get overwhelming and you start to believe you can't do it, turn to God and seek His Word and will. He will reveal the truth to you through His scripture or the still small voice of the Holy Spirit. Also, you may want to take the time to share with a trusted friend who won't give you advice but that will let you talk things out without judgment. Share with someone who understands that what God wants from you is for you to trust Him and walk with Him.

Don't get caught up in the troubles of this world or focus on your own discomfort. Focus on His truth and how He could perhaps work through you today. More challenges will come and more obstacles will pop up but you are not alone, nor are you ill equipped.

Ephesians 5:17–18, 19 "Don't act thoughtlessly, but understand what the Lord wants you to do. Don't be drunk with wine, because that will ruin your life. Instead, be filled with the Holy Spirit, singing psalms and hymns and spiritual songs among yourselves, and making music to the Lord in your hearts."

- What are some of your own automatic, thoughtless responses or actions that don't serve you well?
- When you act thoughtlessly, what happens?
- What causes you to act thoughtlessly? (Remember, we are responsible for our actions so an answer of "because he was an idiot" does not count. You need to dig a little deeper.)

Isaiah 40:31 "But those who trust in the Lord will find new strength. They will soar high on wings like eagles. They will run and not grow weary. They will walk and not faint."

- What vision does this ignite in you?
- Will you ask for help if you need it?

Romans 12:16 "If it is possible, as much as depends on you, live peaceably with all men."

- Why is this difficult for us?
- What is important to God, what does He want?

Romans 13:8 "Owe no one anything except to love one another, for he who loves another has fulfilled the law."

Romans 8:5-9 "...those who are controlled by the Holy Spirit think about things that please the spirit. So letting your sinful nature control your mind leads to death...you are controlled by the spirit if you have the spirit of God living in you."

- What will you miss out on by letting go of your behaviors that feed your flesh? What do you feel like when you give up the wine/chocolate/shopping...?
- What do you need God to replace for you? I may need to let go of gossip, but it feeds my sense of importance. I need God to show me how important I am to Him. I need to feel loved.

One day, while trail riding with my husband, he asked me to take the lead. At first I wasn't sure if I wanted to; there was a sense of safety riding behind him. I trusted him. He patiently encouraged me and told me that it would help me. Since I trusted his judgment, I agreed, and I did in fact grow. I grew so much over the course of the next few rides. My confidence increased, my sense of excitement returned and I reached a new level. By keeping an open mind, trusting my partner and trying outside my comfort zone, I grew to a level I had no idea was even an option.

There was a time our relationship was broken beyond repair. Thankfully, through the guidance from our God and trusted counsel of Godly friends, we forgave each other completely and we received our healing miracle.

Physical Health

1 Corinthians 6:19 "Or do you not know that your body is a temple of the Holy Spirit who is in you, whom you have from God, and that you are not your own? For you have been bought with a price: therefore glorify God in your body."

Over the past few chapters, you've had the opportunity to analyze behaviors and attitudes that impact your emotional health. Now, it is time to consciously focus on how these same behaviors and attitudes impact your physical health. Some people may replace one addiction for another (food for alcohol or shopping for sex) and some people over- eat due to stress, while others may avoid food at all costs during stressful times. Is your relationship with food and fitness healthy? How would you define healthy in this area? (For me it means that my intake is balanced and in moderation; it means food doesn't control me. I choose what and when to eat. It means I exercise as scheduled and with specific goals in mind.)

Are you an emotional eater? Do you crave sweets regularly? It didn't take long for me to realize that I had to address some unhealthy and often subconscious behaviors.

I encourage you to spend time with your Heavenly Father and seek His wisdom. Ask Him to help you identify your struggles and strongholds. Be sure you have the power of the Holy

Spirit behind you so complete success is a loving process of awareness and acceptance

It is important that you pay attention to your behaviors when food is involved. If you are overeating ask yourself if you are "stuffing your feelings"? Are you angry, sad, mad, bitter or bored? Are you punishing yourself for some offense? Are you eating to feel better? Are you obsessively not eating?

Take some time and identify the causes. I have struggled with sweets when I'm stressed out. When I slowed down and paid attention to what I was thinking or feeling, I realized I was repeating what I heard as a child, "eat, you'll feel better". I'm sure it was not the intent of my grandmother to plant that seed, but that is the one that stuck. It is imperative to identify your triggers. One of my triggers for overeating and drinking was my lack of control over some situations.

Uncomfortable feelings of any manner and I would react. That was all it took before I quickly spiraled out of control. What I can do now is slow down and pay attention to how I'm feeling. Then, choose a healthier option that will give me the same results. Instead of mindlessly grabbing something, I may take a 10 minute break with a cup of tea. At first I didn't believe it would help, but my healthy alternatives do work once I choose what is mine and practice it.

I know. I know… it seems like a lot of work and so difficult. It is. Getting healthy and aligning your emotional and spiritual health with your physical health takes work. It is WORTH IT. Do not give up on yourself. This is an important piece of the puzzle. Once you identify your triggers and your response, it is time, again, to take responsibility.

Over the course of this study, you've learned to be honest with yourself and others. You've learned to journal and you've learned to let go and forgive. You've also learned about self –

responsibility. Remember we are in charge of how we feel. On purpose, we do not give that away to anyone. Think about it, take your time and own it.

FOOD IMPACTS MOOD

It's time to start putting that pen into practice.

- How are your thoughts connected to your emotions, connected to your actions impacting you?
- What can you do to remain in charge of how you feel?
- What area regarding your physical wellbeing needs attention and discipline?
- What foods do you eat? (Lean protein and fresh clean vegetables and whole grains?)
- Do you stretch and practice deep breathing?
- Are you able to understand what your body is telling you or do you notice your body's response to these behaviors or lack of?
- Are you exercising regularly?

It is time to record some of the consequences you've endured due to "giving in." It is always easier to change a behavior when we acknowledge it and it is easier to acknowledge it when it is in black and white.

If God is leading you to address this issue, what is the conviction He is using? Is it your weight? Record it. Is it how you feel when you climb a flight of stairs? Record it. Admit the ways you "give in" so you are also aware of what not to do anymore. Are you feeling uncomfortable? Good... It is time to be bold and confident and face reality head on – what needs to change?

While exercise is great, physical well-being is truly made in the kitchen. If you eat a lot of sugar and refined foods, you will be sluggish and generally feel "yucky." If you eat clean, i.e., lean protein, lots of green leafy veggies and fruits and complex carbohydrates, you will be energized and look bright.

I encourage you to make slow deliberate changes to your daily meals. Don't start with restrictions. Begin with a commitment to be sure you are eating 5 servings of vegetables a day. Commit to eating lean proteins at every meal. Drink plenty of clean water.

It is so much easier to say no to things we don't need when we aren't hungry and wanting. If you decide to get rid of sugar... that's best cold turkey. It is hard, but trust me, you will feel a world better after the first week. Be encouraged and find some accountability partners. (For more information on healthy eating, there are hundreds of free sites with great ideas. You will surely find something to suit your taste and your life style).

As far as physical fitness is concerned, I am all for it. In fact, this is one area that I have so much practice in experiencing the benefits, it's hard for me not to exercise. Figure out what activities your body is naturally good at and do it regularly. Don't get caught up in fads. Do what you like to do and do it on most days.

If you are looking to see results (lose fat/gain muscle), you have to be consistent. You will have to get uncomfortable, frequently. Your exercise plan does not include whatever activity you do throughout the day. Exercise is an activity you are doing specifically for the health and fitness of your heart, lungs and muscles. Of course, as with all exercise programs, it is important to check with your health care provider before beginning.

You are right where you are supposed to be. Keep moving forward. Please don't expect yourself to create huge changes in every area, all at once. Do your best; focus where you are called to focus and then press on. On days you don't feel like walking out your recovery, whether it's exercising, eating right, or journaling, push through. You won't regret it. Keep yourself accountable. When that little voice in your head says, "I don't feel like it," quickly respond with "Who asked you?" You will overcome the "I can't do it" and the "I don't want to" chorus in time. With time and self-discipline you will gain momentum; and gaining momentum in this area will prove valuable.

1 Corinthians 6:20 "For you were bought at a price, therefore glorify God in your body and in your spirit, which are God's."

Mark 2:27 "The Sabbath was made for man, not man for the Sabbath."

Now I know we've gone over a lot, and there is a lot of work in self-healing, but it is always important to recognize that it will all be for naught if we do not rest and rejuvenate regularly. It is common that most people become vulnerable when they are overtired. It is a common place to fall into the traps of the devil.

When we work beyond the fatigue, our family suffers, our marriage suffers and all aspects of our health suffer. Can you see how this situation is a set up for a devil's playground? Fighting and misunderstandings at home tempt us to fall back into old habits. Before Jesus left, He commanded us to "love one another." How can we love others when we don't love ourselves?

We are the hands and feet of Jesus. We are called into fellowship with others. If we are striving to live how Jesus lived, we are called to serve others; care for the orphans, widows and poor. We need to heed the still small voice of God when He whispers, "Stop, rest, be done." I know it is difficult. We have been taught that it is selfish to take time for ourselves. However, my friend, it is selfish for us to grow weary and ragged and bitter in service.

If we have no love, peace or joy stored up inside of us, how can we possibly share it? You've run on empty before; imagine how empowering it will feel to run on full! Imagine how much more you can do and how much more you will enjoy serving if you are rested. Honor your time of rest not because you are weak and frail, but because we are strong enough to pay attention.

- What is the Sabbath and how would it help you to honor the day?
- What would one entire day completely off look like for you?

FATIGUE

Fatigue leads to mistakes. A couple weeks ago while riding with my husband, I decided to push myself harder than ever, not because I wanted to for me, but because I had the thought that my husband was not getting a hard enough workout riding with me – so many lessons in this thought.

I was powering through the trails like a machine, the crunch of my tires on the ground and the warm breeze on my face just encouraged me to push harder, even as fatigue began to set in. As I came up to a pretty tight turn I squeezed the brakes, only I squeezed them too hard and fast. To clarify, my bike stopped, I didn't. Not only did I squeeze too tight, but I squeezed the wrong hand and put on my front brake. Although I looked really cool with mud all over me and blood dripping down my arm, I made a very dangerous mistake.

My husband rode up behind me and said, "You are getting too tired; we need to stop." While I knew he was right, I got angry. I didn't want to be tired, more accurately; I didn't want to admit I was tired. My best isn't good when I'm that tired and sometimes I don't even realize it. When I start to feel over-whelmed, frustrated or inadequate, that's my cue and, thank God, I'm finally starting to listen.

Read 1 Samuel 14:24–29 "My father made trouble for us all"… "a command like that only hurts us. See how refreshed I am now" There is a lot of …"

Look up and read the above scripture in full and let it sink in. This is a long one so you will need to put me down and pick up the book I keep referring to. King Saul hastily declared a rule for this particular battle that would harm his men. He didn't go before God and ask the Lord if this is what He wanted. People often do this to themselves without thinking; then our lack of success leaves us worse off than where we started.

Perhaps we started a fast without considering the implications on our life or schedule. Then when we can't achieve it, we may heap guilt and shame on themselves and fall into the trap of old coping skills. Sometimes when we are asking God why we can't be better at something we want to be good at, we may have to be prepared for Him to say "because I never asked you to do that".

When I was growing up there were many things I learned that were only half true or it was a belief, but it was not grounded in scripture. It was no one's fault; it's just how they were taught. Now, I take the time to search out the truth whenever I have doubt. I allow the Holy Spirit to reveal the truth of God's Word to me. This leads to where God wants me, joyfully free.

Lamentations 3:25-26 "The Lord is good to those who depend on Him. To those who search for Him. So it is good to wait quietly for salvation from the Lord."

How comfortable are you sitting quietly with the Lord? Why?

Matthew 11: 28-30 "Then Jesus said 'Come to me, all who are weary and carry heavy burdens, and I will give you rest. Take my yoke upon you. Let me teach you, because I am humble and gentle at heart, and you will find rest for your souls. For my yoke is easy to bear, and the burden I give you is light."

ENCOURAGEMENT

When we are able to stay committed to our self-care habits, a little missed sleep or one poor dietary choice won't hurt too much. Poor choices over time will take us out. Daily quiet time with God, healthy fuel, clean water, adequate rest, sunlight, laughter, keeping our priorities clear and our boundaries healthy will help us sail over the daily roots, gullies and obstacles that are guaranteed in life.

He tells us He will never leave us; He does not say everything will be fun and easy. He tells us we can trust Him and lean on Him and walk with Him every day and everywhere. He keeps His promise and we have to do our part with choosing healthy options and healthy relationships. We are tasked with this body; at what level we care for it is up to us. If you hate to exercise, hire a trainer to help. If you don't know what a healthy dinner looks like, do some research.

Our physical, emotional, spiritual and mental health are all connected. So when one area improves, we tend to see some improvement in the other areas, use this advantage. If exercise or diet is a stronghold for you, grow. Begin the journey to own the responsibility of caring for your body.

APPLICATION

The other day I noticed I was having an easier time exercising. I lost five pounds of body fat and really felt the difference. Losing five pounds of water and losing five pounds of fat is a big difference. In fact, I was all but certain I added lean muscle while I lost weight. It was awesome. I was strong, efficient and solid, yet I was lighter. As a trail rider, this translated to exceptional rides. Being strong gave me endurance and the ability to build on a steady, powerful cadence that propelled me over challenging obstacles and allowed me to navigate gullies and roots with ease.

Losing weight (fat) and gaining muscle empowered me to find the "sweet spot" crucial to a great ride. The confidence of my increased strength and endurance kept me focused on the ride; relaxed shoulders, steady gaze ahead and strong full circles with my legs.

It is truly remarkable how one area – body, mind or spirit – makes a difference in the other areas, for the good or the bad. So, as my spirit aligns with God's will, it is easier to make healthy decisions in my daily walk.

My dear sister, be encouraged. This is your journey. Some days are easy and everything goes well while other days seem like abysmal failures. Pick yourself up, dust off and hop back on the bike of life. You are victorious.

Jeremiah 33:6 "Nevertheless, I will bring health and healing to it; I will heal my people and will let them enjoy abundant peace and security."

Perseverance

Romans 2:7 "to those who by perseverance in doing good seek for glory and honor and immortality, eternal life..."

Oh perseverance, a beautiful word that signifies strength, hope and longsuffering. Say it and visions of struggles and trials come to mind. Maybe a faint smile crosses your lips as you recall everything you've overcome. Be encouraged special one. You are strong and mighty in the Lord. You have overcome hardships and heartache. You are victorious. Your story is still being written. Your journey is not over. In fact, you will be walking out this journey and growing until the day you meet Jesus.

As you find momentum in our spiritual walk, your desire to maintain a healthy lifestyle will grow. Changes in our lifestyle require time to take hold. Focus on your positive behaviors and positive self-talk. Remember, nothing worth having is easy; and be patient. In our microwave culture, it is easy to grow weary when things don't happen "NOW."

I'm smiling to myself as I think of my struggles and unrealistic expectations in the area of healthy eating. After a couple of days of no sugar, lean meats, complex carbohydrates and exercising, I hop on the scale expecting "as seen on T.V." results. When I don't get the results I want (and expect, come on... the girl said I'd drop 20 pounds!), I get discouraged. Heck, sometimes I am tempted to even sabotage my best efforts. Then I am reminded that I belong to the God of the universe. I am His and He promises to do a good work in me until the day of Christ Jesus' return. I am on a journey.

Remember, God is much more interested in the condition of our heart than He is our circumstance. All you have to do is read the Bible to see that God uses sinful, broken people to positively impact the lives of those around them. As you read His living word, allow it to realign your life to His will. He is doing a good work in you whether or not you see it or "feel" it. Do your part and He will do His. Persevere.

Struggling with the unlovable? He understands. It is not our natural tendency to love our enemies. It's not natural to turn the other cheek. It's difficult to forgive. Start small and just practice. You can practice loving people who are tough to love. Practice forgiving and experience the freedom that comes with it. Frankly, I would have given up on me a long time ago. It took time and practice to learn to forgive and love myself unconditionally.

You want a tough one? The person at work that is so difficult for you to be around? Pray for them every morning for two weeks and see what happens. I know it's not easy; if it were easy, we wouldn't grow from it; we wouldn't benefit from it.

When conflict occurs or someone is simply being difficult, it's okay not to engage. I have had much success simply allowing someone to finish what they started. I don't engage, I let them talk, in front of me or behind my back – it's all good. Let it pass, don't give it energy, forgive quickly and it's amazing how it simply vanishes.

When someone wants to fight and has no one to fight with, it loses its usefulness. You don't have extra energy to spend on trivial matters. Let it go, move forward and chase God. After a couple times, this is not difficult at all. The joy of a healthy response to our heavenly, loving Father is so fulfilling.

On this journey you will learn that pleasing God benefits you more than it benefits God. Instead of finding momentary comfort in your weaknesses, unhealthy reactions and bad habits, you are finding real joy and amazing peace from your time with God.

The goal of walking out your healing is to develop the fruits of the Holy Spirit in your life. *Galatians 5:22 "But the fruit of the Spirit is love, joy, peace, forbearance, kindness, goodness, faithfulness, gentleness and self-control."* Through the Holy Spirit you are no longer in bondage to your sin and old behaviors. Gain momentum in the matters of your heart through study, prayer and meditation no matter what your circumstances; the freedom will amaze you.

Galatians 6:7-8 "You will always harvest what you plant. Those who live only to satisfy their own sinful nature will harvest decay and death..."

- What are you harvesting in your life right now?
- What have you harvested in the past and what has it produced?

Romans 6:11 "Likewise you also, reckon yourselves to be dead indeed to sin, but alive to God in Christ Jesus our Lord."

- What does it mean for you to be dead to your sin?
- What did Jesus die for as it pertains to your life?

Lamentations 3:25-26 Jeremiah said, "The Lord is good to those who depend on Him, to those who search for Him. So it is good to wait quietly for salvation from the Lord"

- What can you do when you get impatient and frustrated?

- What are some expectations you have? Are you able to release them over to our Lord and trust Him with the results?

REALIGNING OUR PRIORITIES

If you asked a close friend what your most important priority was, what would they say? What do you say is the most important thing in your life? Is it your children, your job, your walk with God? Does what you say match up with your actions?

I would say with all certainty that, before, my children topped my Most Important list followed by my fitness level, my career and my home life.

I put nothing before them and that didn't work. My intentions were good but my priorities were messed up. It took a while for me to understand that my children were not going to be "OK" unless my husband and I were "OK" and we were never going to be "OK" if we didn't start putting our relationship with God and each other before them. Thankfully, my husband also realized that his walk with God needed to be first in his life.

It is not easy. In fact, my priorities shifted quite a bit as I began to grow. For now, my top three or four are solid and don't change. Once I get to five or six, it varies according to what's happening. A recent move adjusted my fitness plans for a month. Having priorities is not meant to be strict or rigid, it's meant to help you align your decision making with what's important to you with God.

EXERCISE

Remember when we started this journey I promised that you would have some work to do? Well, I am living up to that promise. It's time to analyze a few things:

- Look at your checkbook and credit card statements. Where do you spend your hard earned money?
- Look at your calendar. What do you do with your free time?

Look at where your priorities are now and where you would like them to be. If this is the first time you are doing this exercise, I imagine, like most people, there are a few adjustments that can be made.

This kind of adjustment in our life makes a big difference. It puts lives in alignment so there is no wasted time or energy and less chance to be pulled off track. Remember, we don't walk by feelings. Feeling good is not always an indicator of how we are actually doing. For example, if a high priority is my physical health but I still spend money and time on smoking then it is obvious I need to get serious and quit. If I spend a few days without smoking, I will be doing great but may not "feel" great. In fact I'm sure I would feel awful!

Getting over the pull of instant gratification and the frequently overwhelming discomforts that accompany battling an addiction can feel like torture. It is important that we focus on truth. The truth is it will pass and it will get better. So even though I may *feel* horrible while I detox from cigarettes, or sugar, or whatever, the fact is, I am *doing* great. Get it?

There will always be an effort required to overcome our fleshly desires, especially when it will result in growth. God knows the struggles you are up against, He sent His Son to clear your path and the Holy Spirit to live in you. Let Him lead your journey. Don't forget to ask for help when you need it. Set your priorities and identify the patterns that may be holding you back; then, align your strength with His and ride on.

- Can you identify any patterns or behaviors that are not lined up with your priorities?
- What do you plan to do about it?
- What could someone do to support you?
- Who do you think could support you without crossing any healthy boundary?

As you grow in your walk with God, are set free from your strongholds, and restore broken relationships, you will face many challenges and attacks. While I don't know where you are in your walk with the Lord, I pray that you are aware that there is a spiritual battle that goes on around us.

> Ephesians 6:12-13 *"For our struggle is not against flesh and blood, but against the rulers, against the authorities, against the powers of this dark world and against the spiritual forces of evil in the heavenly realms. Therefore put on the full armor of God, so that when the day of evil comes, you may be able to stand your ground, and after you have done everything, to stand."*

You see, the enemy of your soul is out to kill, steal and destroy. He doesn't want you walking in freedom. He doesn't want your marriage to survive. He doesn't want you to become an effective leader or parent. No, he wants you to live in defeat. In defeat you are no threat to him.

Beloved, do not fear. You were not given a spirit of fear, but of power. 2 Timothy 1:17 *"For the Spirit God gave us does not make us timid, but gives us power, love and self-discipline."*

Be aware. The enemy is subtle and personal. While he can't read your mind, he knows your struggles. He is a liar and he knows how to dress things up so that they are attractive to you.

With awareness, his lies don't sound so appealing. For example, as you are getting ready for church and everything seems to go wrong, you will be tempted to stay home and crawl back into bed.

It is when you know the right thing to eat but a little voice gives you a "better," less healthy option that is so attractive. It happens when you are writing a book to share what God can do and a voice says "what do you know?" When you are applying for your dream job and you suddenly feel inadequate and insecure.

The enemy does not want you to be successful and healthy. When you are healthy, you are much harder to trap. Physical exercise helps us in every way, so he would rather you watched TV, have a glass of wine or gossip with friends. Be aware.

It is so much easier to believe a lie when it is cloaked in truth. The enemy will use things like your past experience, what you've been taught as a child or perhaps what society says as truth. You've heard the lie before, perhaps out of a parent's mouth even, so why wouldn't you believe it to be true? "You are not strong enough hold that kind of job." Or "You've never been able to quit before, why now?"– Challenge these defeating statements. I beg you, challenge them! You are a child of the King; you can do or be much more than you give yourself credit. "Drug addicts always go back, you can never trust them" – really? Have you met Jesus? He is a healer, He is a provider and He is our brother. Identify your defeating thoughts and challenge them.

Amos 7:7-8 The prophet Amos recorded this vision "I saw the Lord standing beside a wall that had been built using a plumb line. He was using a plumb line to see if it was still straight. And the Lord said..."I will test my people with this plumb line"

- What are you measuring truth against?
- What is your plumb line?
- Where can we turn to find out if what we are thinking is from our God or from the enemy?

Since Tom and I got back together there are certain things we identified as being healthy for our relationship. One of these is going for a walk after work. It is neutral territory that gives us an interruption free opportunity to share our day.

Sometimes, after work, we are emotionally tired or stressed and don't feel like going. We could easily justify sitting on the couch, but the truth is we need the walk to reenergize our lives. It keeps us connected to each other and it keeps us aware of our priorities. This doesn't mean we never skip a walk. It means we are aware that we have an enemy that hates every healthy thing we do. It means we are aware that we are no match for this enemy apart from God.

We have already tried doing life with us at the center of it. It did not work out, at all. With God at the center of our lives, we are free to walk in the love, peace and truth of the Holy Spirit.

Power, Love & Self-Discipline

Ecclesiastes 7:8 "The end of a matter is better than its beginning, and patience is better than pride."

My dear sister, I encourage you to meditate on this scripture recognizing the truth of the Living Word. God loves you beyond measure. He is your Redeemer, Deliverer, Healer and Provider. If you only take one thing from this book, I urge you to seek God with all of your heart. Seek Him and you will find peace that transcends all understanding.

As you continue on this journey, be aware that the presence of sin in our lives keeps us from a pure, healthy, dynamic and enriching relationship with God, and others. God is a gentleman. He will not impose Himself on us. We have free will to choose. Remember – sin pulls us from God. It is a slippery slope; and before we even know what happened, we have compromised our way out of God's presence.

While we may realize it late, it is never *too* late. Run back to Him, RUN. He is solid and doesn't change, His word does not falter, it is as relevant to our lives today as it was to our ancestors. The Bible is crazy supernatural, it doesn't make sense how two people can read the same thing and receive something so different. I can't express how much I wish everyone could see it for what it is, but you won't see it without a relationship with Him.

You are blind until the Holy Spirit gives you sight.

We are called to do life in fellowship with others. Luke 10:26 Jesus said, *"Love the Lord your God with all your heart and with all your soul and with all your strength and with all your mind'; and, 'Love your neighbor as yourself.'"*

This is important. Love is what it's all about. By learning how to love Him, and then each other, we become who He created us to be. Then why are our journeys so different, so unique and individual? I don't know. Why does everyone's brokenness and healing look so different? Sorry, I don't know. However, I do know it doesn't help to judge others simply because their "mess up" looks different than ours.

I know it takes love, time and discernment to get better. We all need to identify the dysfunctional and balance the healthy. If you feel as though you have strongholds that are impossible to break, reach out to a trusted believer who understands your struggle. Perhaps someone who has had victory in that same area. It will help in your quest for deliverance.

If your marriage is broken, face it and address it. Do not give up on it. Smiling and saying everything is fine allows it just to get worse – that's denial. Always surrender and turn to God first for guidance, then move forward as He instructs. You are only responsible for your part. I repeat, we are only responsible for our own thoughts, feelings, actions and behaviors. So keep it simple and just do your best.

Ecclesiastes 4: 9-12 "Two are better than one, because they have a good reward for their labor. For if they fall, one will lift up his companion, But woe to him who is alone when he falls, for he has no one to help him up. Again, if two lie together they will keep warm: But how can one be warm alone? Though one may be overpowered by another, two can withstand him, a threefold cord is not quickly broken."

- Who makes up your threefold cord?

John 14:27 "I am leaving you with a gift-peace of mind and heart. And the peace I give is a gift the world cannot give. So don't be troubled or afraid."

- What is the difference between the peace that Jesus left us with and the peace in this world?

Deuteronomy 30:19 "Today I have given you the choice between life and death, between blessings and curses. Now I call on Heaven and earth to witness the choice you make. Oh, that you would choose life, so that you and your descendants might live!"

Philippians 4:13 "I can do all things through Christ who strengthens me."

Imagine what you would do if you truly believed you had the strength of God the Father, God the Son and God the Holy Spirit inside you.

- What do you want to do that you don't believe you can?
- What do you think God would have you do in this world for Him and His kingdom?
- What's holding you back?

I encourage you to start walking it out. When you are stressed remind yourself that the Holy Spirit lives in you. Rather than crying out to God for peace, remind yourself that the Holy Spirit is peace, which means it is already in you. Just receive it. Breathe in it. Walk in it.

Did you ever hear the saying "the more I learn the less I know"? That is what this journey feels like to me. I spent so much time trying to figure out why I was sabotaging myself and analyzing the roots of my behaviors, I kept carrying around the baggage. God tells us to let it go. Surrender it.

Hebrews 11:1 "Now faith is confidence in what we hope for and assurance about what we do not see."

There is a wonderful sense of mystery surrounding God. I can't answer most of the questions people ask. How could I? It makes no sense to explain how faith works.

However, I know that when I received the gift of God's Son and accepted His death as forgiveness of my sin, I finally understood that I am saved by grace. And through this grace I am capable of loving and forgiving others for their trespasses against me.

It makes no sense to admit to someone that I just simply couldn't do this life without my relationship with God. It's not that I don't think I could do it. Hear me – I know I couldn't do it. I didn't do it. I would not respond in love. I would not forgive so quickly. I would not be able to give away money and I would not be free from my strongholds. In fact, I would probably still be out searching for "something better" and never be satisfied.

Sweet sister, there is so much to experience. You have just scratched the surface. Your vision for your life pales in comparison to God's vision for your life.

If you are not already, I encourage you to find a church home and get plugged into a family of believers. Spend time talking to God through the Holy Spirit throughout the day. Take wonderful care of yourself; you have permission and an obligation to do so. Rest before you need to. Don't believe anything the enemy has for you; claim Jesus and the Holy Spirit as yours for protection. Keep you and your relationships healthy by keeping love at the center of it.

You have been given a glimpse of what life is like with the guidance of your Heavenly Father through the power of the Holy Spirit.

When I began my journey, my prayer was for my children to not be damaged too badly by the divorce. Sometimes God says yes, sometimes He says maybe later – to me He said "I've got a better idea."

He saved my marriage and my family.

What if you got out of the way and allowed the Holy Spirit to mold you into the woman God created you to be?

APPLICATION

The more I ride over those bridges the more confident I become in my skills. I don't even hesitate; I just push forward. The more challenging sections of the path would have me tense in anticipation; as I learned to navigate them I became comfortable and charged ahead. There are areas that I know I will get better at as long as I don't give up. I keep pushing forward, one area at a time.

When I get uncomfortable or impatient when I don't see progress, I remind myself of the truth, and the truth is, if I am persistent and believe that I will be successful, I will improve. Sometimes I focus on my bigger goals, sometimes I focus on what's in front of me, but I always remain vigilant and disciplined to get where I'm going.

My beloved friend, buckle up, it is quite a ride!

A Letter from Carmela

Thank You for walking part of your journey with me. I am honored and grateful. I thank God every time my pain and my growth are able to help someone. He truly uses everything for His good for those who love Him. I hope and pray this book brought some healing and restoration to you wherever you are in your walk.

I wish we could get together and talk about the amazing things He is doing in your life. The uncanny little stories that can only be God are so uplifting. Like the time my sister MaryAnn was in Haiti and learned the women were hoping for a sewing school. Knowing how much the skill saved her as a single mom she prayed. "God I don't know how to get them machines and supplies; if you want this you need to make it happen." Within months 8 machines had been donated but they needed supplies. Again she prayed. Within one week MaryAnn met a woman who was closing her business. During the discussion she asked MaryAnn if she knew where she could donate a large amount of thread and material. Can you imagine how she felt? It is like we know Him and trust Him, but when He really shows up, it's a bit intimidating and awe inspiring. Be ready – we serve a God of abundance. Believe and be ready. If it is His will, there will be no stopping it. Now that you know God and are beginning to trust Him, I hope you are expecting miracles.

Let's pray together one more time –

Dear Heavenly Father, thank you for the gift of sister-hood. Thank you for the promise to use all for your glory. Thank you for the precious gift of your Son, Jesus Christ, and the indwelling of the Holy Spirit.

Lord, I lift up my sister reading this right now. Father may her heart be softened and eyes opened to your work in her life. May she feel the presence of the Holy Spirit when she rises and when she rests. As she draws near to you Lord, I pray that you will reveal yourself in ways she has never known.

In the precious and holy name of Your Son and Our Savior Jesus Christ, Amen.

Maggie dreams of killing her abusive ex-husband who has threat-
ened to kidnap their young son. As Maggie struggles to put the past
behind her, an early snow storm reveal her worst nightmare, he has
found them and is living in the woods behind their house. Can
Maggie convince the authorities her life is in danger,or will the
memories of her past keep her bound long after Jack is gone?

Evangelist Troy Freeman explains the power our words contain,
power that releases, healing, favor, protection and hope. Take the
journey with this personal account of God's Glory manifesting as
his word is spoken through your mouth and changes every situation
of your life.

CPSIA information can be obtained at www.ICGtesting.com
Printed in the USA
BVOW08s1938080815

411953BV00002BA/46/P